THE LIGHT OF THE WORLD

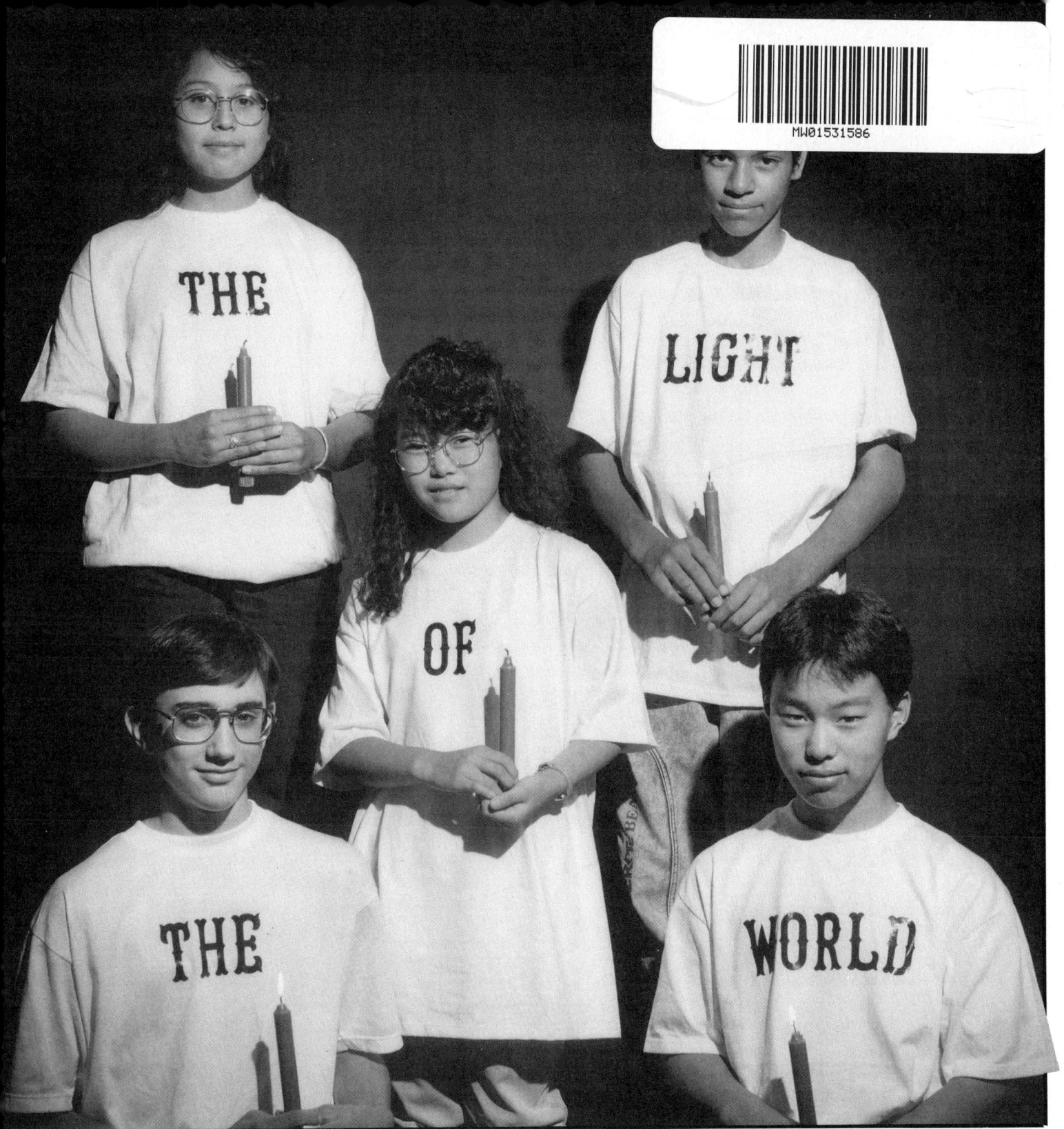

SERMON on the Mount

A 4-week course to help junior highers understand Jesus' teachings on the Beatitudes, the Old Testament laws, prayer and the kingdom life

Group
Loveland, Colorado

by Stephen Parolini

Group's ACTIVE BIBLE CURRICULUM®

Group®

Sermon on the Mount
Copyright © 1992 Group Publishing, Inc.

Credits
Edited by Stephen Parolini
Cover designed by Jill Nordbye and DeWain Stoll
Interior designed by Judy Bienick and Jan Aufdemberge
Illustrations by Raymond Medici
Cover photography by David Priest

ISBN 1-55945-129-7
12 11 10 9 8 7 6 5   04 03 02 01 00 99 98 97
Printed in the United States of America.

CONTENTS

SERMON ON THE MOUNT

Tell junior highers or middle schoolers they're going to study the Sermon on the Mount, and you'll probably get responses like these:

"The Sermon on the Mount? We have to study a sermon? What's the fun in that?"

"Why can't we have an interesting topic?"

"We get sermons every week. We don't need them in Sunday school, too."

It's no surprise kids are turned off by the thought of a study of the Sermon on the Mount. The word "sermon" can turn kids off pretty quickly. But your kids probably *would* dive into discussions about what's important in life, the value of prayer and how to be a good Christian. Well, guess what . . . those are the main issues this course explores!

Teenagers don't always know what they want from Sunday school, but surveys suggest they do want solid training on what it means to be a Christian. And Jesus' teaching in the Sermon on the Mount can give them just what they want.

This course helps junior highers and middle schoolers discover ways to better serve and follow God. Kids will learn that Jesus' teachings about the law of Moses, prayer, money, judging and living a life pleasing to God are just as valid today as they were in New Testament times.

Use *Sermon on the Mount* to help kids apply Jesus' teaching to their everyday lives. With this creative course,

Christian Teenagers and Faith

- 71 percent want to learn how to know and love Jesus.
- 64 percent want to know the Bible and its meaning for their lives.
- 53 percent want to know how to apply their faith to everyday decisions.
- 40 percent want to know how to pray and meditate.

kids can grow closer to God through an exploration of the wonderful lessons Jesus taught his disciples—and teaches us today through the Bible.

By the end of this course, your students will:
● discover what makes people happy;
● learn how Jesus taught a new way of thinking in the Beatitudes;
● discover how it feels to break the rules in an activity;
● discover how Jesus brought new perspectives to Old Testament laws;
● explore Jesus' teaching on prayer;
● learn why it's important not to judge others; and
● commit to follow Jesus' teachings.

COURSE OBJECTIVES

HOW TO USE THIS COURSE

ACTIVE
LEARNING

Think back on an important lesson you've learned in life. Did you learn it from reading about it? from hearing about it? from something you experienced? Chances are, the most important lessons you've learned came from something you've experienced. That's what active learning is—learning by doing. And active learning is a key element in Group's Active Bible Curriculum.

Active learning leads students in doing things that help them understand important principles, messages and ideas. It's a discovery process that helps kids internalize what they learn.

Each lesson section in Group's Active Bible Curriculum plays an important part in active learning:

The **Opener** involves kids in the topic in fun and unusual ways.

The **Action and Reflection** includes an experience designed to evoke specific feelings in the students. This section also processes those feelings through "How did you feel?" questions and applies the message to situations kids face.

The **Bible Application** actively connects the topic with the Bible. It helps kids see how the Bible is relevant to the situations they face.

The **Commitment** helps students internalize the Bible's message and commit to make changes in their lives.

The **Closing** funnels the lesson's message into a time of creative reflection and prayer.

When you put all the sections together, you get a lesson that's fun to teach. And kids get messages they'll remember.

**BEFORE THE
4-WEEK
SESSION**

● Read the Introduction, the Course Objectives and This Course at a Glance.

● Decide how you'll publicize the course using the clip art on the Publicity Page (p. 9). Prepare fliers, newsletter articles and posters as needed.

● Look at the Bonus Ideas (p. 46) and decide which ones you'll use.

• Read the opening statements, Objectives and Bible Basis for the lesson. The Bible Basis shows how specific passages relate to junior highers and middle schoolers today.

• Choose which Opener and Closing options to use. Each is appropriate for a different kind of group.

• Gather necessary supplies from This Lesson at a Glance.

• Read each section of the lesson. Adjust where necessary for your class size and meeting room.

• The approximate minutes listed give you an idea of how long each activity will take. Each lesson is designed to take 35 to 60 minutes. Shorten or lengthen activities as needed to fit your group.

• If you see you're going to have extra time, do an activity or two from the "If You Still Have Time . . ." box or from the Bonus Ideas (p. 46).

• Dive into the activities with the kids. Don't be a spectator. The lesson will be more successful and rewarding to both you and your students.

• Though some kids may at first think certain activities are "silly," they'll enjoy them, and they'll remember the messages from these activities long after the lesson is over. As one Active Bible Curriculum user has said, "I can ask the kids questions about a lesson I did three weeks ago, and they actually remember what I taught!" And that's the whole idea of teaching . . . isn't it?

Have fun with the activities you lead. Remember, it is Jesus who encourages us to become "like little children." Besides, how often do your kids get *permission* to express their childlike qualities?

HELPFUL HINTS

• The answers given after discussion questions are responses your students *might* give. They aren't the only answers or the "right" answers. If needed, use them to spark discussion. Kids won't always say what you wish they'd say. That's why some of the responses given are negative or controversial. If someone responds negatively, don't be shocked. Accept the person and use the opportunity to explore other angles of the issue.

THIS COURSE AT A GLANCE

Before you dive into the lessons, familiarize yourself with each lesson aim. Then read the scripture passages.
- Study them as a background to the lessons.
- Use them as a basis for your personal devotions.
- Think about how they relate to kids' circumstances today.

LESSON 1: BLESSED ARE . . .

Lesson Aim: To help junior highers understand how the Beatitudes apply to us today.

Bible Basis: 1 Samuel 16:7 and Matthew 5:1-16.

LESSON 2: NEW LIGHT

Lesson Aim: To help junior highers discover how Jesus brought a new light to God's Old Testament laws.

Bible Basis: Jeremiah 31:31-34 and Matthew 5:17-48.

LESSON 3: PRAYER

Lesson Aim: To help junior highers learn how to pray as Jesus taught his disciples to pray.

Bible Basis: Psalm 145:18-19; Matthew 6:5-15; and Matthew 7:7-11.

LESSON 4: THE KINGDOM LIFE

Lesson Aim: To help junior highers learn how to live according to God's ways.

Bible Basis: Matthew 6:19—7:6 and Matthew 7:13-29.

PUBLICITY PAGE

Grab your junior highers' attention! Photocopy this page, then cut out and paste the clip art of your choice in your church bulletin or newsletter to advertise this course on the Sermon on the Mount. Or photocopy and use the ready-made flier as a bulletin insert. Permission to photocopy this clip art is granted for local church use.

Splash the clip art on posters, fliers or even postcards! Just add the vital details: the date and time the course begins and where you'll meet.

It's that simple.

THE LIGHT OF THE WORLD

SERMON on the Mount

SERMON on the Mount

THE LIGHT OF THE WORLD

SERMON on the Mount

A 4-week junior high and middle school course on Jesus' teachings.

Come to _____

On _____

At _____

Come learn how Jesus' Sermon on the Mount applies to *your* life!

BLESSED ARE ...

The Beatitudes introduced a whole new way of thinking to Jesus' disciples and the multitudes who sat with them for Jesus' teaching. Jesus taught that the poor and weak—not the rich and strong—are blessed. This twist of thinking probably surprised many people in Jesus' day. And it also helped people know that God loves each of us—not for what we have, but for who we are. This message can surprise and encourage many junior highers today.

To help junior highers understand how the Beatitudes apply to us today.

LESSON AIM

Students will:
- **discover what makes people happy;**
- **learn how Jesus taught a new way of thinking in the Beatitudes;**
- **explore the meaning of the Beatitudes for today; and**
- **commit to be the light of the world.**

OBJECTIVES

Look up the following scriptures. Then read the background paragraphs to see how the passages relate to your junior highers and middle schoolers.

1 Samuel 16:7 tells how God looks at the heart, not the outward appearance.

In the scriptures leading up to this verse, Samuel was looking for someone to replace Saul as king. In the battle-filled times Samuel lived in, it probably made sense that the next king would be strong and tall—a true warrior to lead the people to many victories. But God helped Samuel discover that outward appearance isn't as important as what's "inside" someone's heart.

This event predated Jesus' Sermon on the Mount by hundreds of years. But God's message to Samuel is similar, in both its freshness and truth, to the words Jesus spoke in the Beatitudes. Junior highers today can learn a great lesson

BIBLE BASIS
1 SAMUEL 16:7
MATTHEW 5:1-16

from this passage as they seek to discover what's truly important in life.

In **Matthew 5:1-16**, Jesus teaches the Beatitudes.

The Sermon on the Mount wasn't intended to present a message of eternal life, but to help people see the way of righteous living. Jesus probably shocked listeners into a new way of thinking as he pointed out the blessedness of the "poor in spirit" and the "merciful."

Our society today preaches the importance of wealth and power. Jesus' message in the Beatitudes—as valid today as when he spoke it—may surprise some junior highers and middle schoolers. Today's kids can be challenged by this message to pursue a righteous way of living instead of riches.

THIS LESSON AT A GLANCE

Section	Minutes	What Students Will Do	Supplies
Opener (Option 1)	5 to 10	**Happy Feet**—Play a game and discover what makes people happy.	
(Option 2)		**Can't Buy Happiness**—Compete to "purchase" the most happiness from each other.	Paper plates, markers, pennies, candy or doughnuts
Action and Reflection	15 to 20	**New Way of Thinking**—Discover how Jesus taught a new way of thinking with the Beatitudes.	Paper, pencils
Bible Application	10 to 15	**What's a Beatitude?**—Explore the meaning of the Beatitudes for the disciples and for today.	Bibles
Commitment	5 to 10	**Light of the World**—Commit to be the light of the world.	"Light in a Dark World" handouts (p. 20), flashlight or candle and matches
Closing (Option 1)	up to 5	**Pass the Salt**—Share "salt" phrases with each other.	Salt
(Option 2)		**More Blessings**—Tell each other ways they're blessed by God.	Bible

The Lesson

☐ OPTION 1: HAPPY FEET

Form a circle. Say: **Today we're going to explore happiness. To begin, I'll call out a list of activities and ask you to respond by indicating whether each activity makes you happy. But instead of indicating your agreement by simply saying "yes" or raising your hand, you'll each perform some crazy physical action. So take a minute to decide what you'll do to indicate your agreement. It's best to make your actions outrageous or silly. For example, if I call out "shopping at the mall" and that activity makes you happy, you might jump up and down while flapping your arms.**

Demonstrate a crazy action for the group. If they laugh, that's great! Kids will feel better about being silly if you set the example of silliness for them.

Give kids a minute to decide on their physical action. Then read the "Happy Actions" list (in the margin) and get kids' reactions. When you finish reading the list, have kids call out other activities and respond to them.

After a few minutes, ask:

● **How did you feel as you watched everyone doing a silly action during this activity?** (It was fun; I had a good time; I was embarrassed.)

● **Did you have fun during this activity? Explain.** (Yes, I liked watching everyone do something silly; no, I was embarrassed.)

● **What did you discover about the things that make people happy?** (We each like different things; people are happy when they get things.)

Say: **Some of you may've had fun doing this activity and others might not have enjoyed it at all. As we've discovered, happiness means different things to different people. Though we pursue happiness in different ways, we all want to be happy—at least some of the time.**

When Jesus first began to preach to his disciples and the multitudes who followed him, he talked about blessedness, which means happiness. But Jesus surprised people by what he said. He didn't say, "Happy are the wealthy and powerful" but instead described people who were "poor in spirit" or "merciful." Let's see if Jesus' message surprises you too.

HAPPY ACTIONS
● going shopping with friends
● winning a part in a school play
● helping a friend succeed in school
● finding a $50 bill
● winning a relay race
● being told you're a great person
● watching your favorite sports team win an important game
● being chosen to sing a solo in choir
● helping a friend overcome depression
● showing mercy to someone who's wronged you
● winning a new car in a national contest

☐ OPTION 2: CAN'T BUY HAPPINESS

Form teams of no more than four. Give teams each four paper plates, a marker and 10 pennies. Have teams each brainstorm four things that make people happy (such as "winning a game" or "getting straight A's") and write one item on each of their paper plates. Then have kids draw smiley faces on the plates.

Say: **The object of this activity is to purchase the most "happiness"—that is, paper plates—from other teams using only your 10 pennies. The team that has the most paper plates at the end of the activity will be the winner and will get this prize. Hold up a food prize such as candy bars or doughnuts. You may bargain however you choose and may offer as few or as many pennies as you want to get the paper plates.**

After three or four minutes, call time. Determine the winning team, if there is one, and award the prize. Kids may have decided not to trade at all. That's okay. If kids didn't trade, have them discuss why.

Have teams read aloud the messages on the paper plates they ended up with. If no team wins, distribute the prize among the whole group.

Then form a circle and ask:

● **How did you feel as you tried to buy other teams' happiness?** (It wasn't easy; no one wanted to sell.)

● **How is that like the way you feel when you try to find happiness in real life?** (I get frustrated; it's different because I don't try to buy happiness.)

● **Can you buy happiness in real life? Explain.** (Yes, you can buy things that make you feel good; no, happiness doesn't come from things you own.)

Say: **You discovered in this activity that it's not easy to "buy" happiness. Yet our society believes that happiness is based on wealth, prestige and power—and things you can buy. In the Sermon on the Mount, Jesus probably surprised the multitudes by describing certain people as "blessed," which means happy. Some versions of the Bible actually use the word "happy" instead of "blessed." Let's see if Jesus' message would surprise people today—and discover how it applies to us.**

Note: Encourage your kids to read Matthew 5—7 during this course. Give a copy of the "Contract and Reading Guide" (p. 19) to students at the beginning or end of today's session. Have kids each read and sign the contract portion—then tear it off and give it to you. Check up on kids' reading progress each week.

NEW WAY OF THINKING

Form teams of no more than five. Give teams each a sheet of paper and a pencil. Say: **I'm going to call out instructions for you to follow, but not in the order I want the instructions followed. Your job is to figure out the meaning of a clue I'll give you, then perform the actions in the proper order.**

I'm going to tell you the instructions only twice, so you'll want to write them on a sheet of paper. When you think your team has figured out the correct order of the instructions, come over to me and perform the tasks. I'll tell you if you get them right. If you're having trouble with the clue, just guess and try your actions in a different order. Here's the clue: Five is nothing, and after four wear a hat on your feet to find order.

Read the following instructions (including the numbers) aloud twice. Pause to allow kids to copy what you say onto their papers. You might need to repeat the clue too. This is supposed to be confusing for kids. Be prepared for puzzled looks and inactivity.

1. **Sing "Row, Row, Row Your Boat" once.**
2. **Give everyone in your group a hug.**
3. **Imitate farm animals.**
4. **Run in place.**
5. **Give your teammates high fives.**
6. **Do two jumping jacks.**
7. **Tell what you like most about your teammates.**
8. **Bark like dogs.**

The correct order of actions is 1, 2, 3, 4, 8, 7, 6 (#5 isn't to be completed). The clue suggests that action #5 shouldn't be done (is "nothing") and that after doing the first four actions kids should do the next three in reverse order.

It's possible kids won't figure out the clue. That's okay. After a few tries or when kids begin to get frustrated, call time. If a team does figure out the code, congratulate that team and have them tell what they did to figure it out. Otherwise, explain the clue yourself.

Ask:

● **How did you feel as you tried to understand the clue?** (I was frustrated; confused; challenged.)

● **How might that be like the way the disciples felt as they tried to understand Jesus' teaching in the Sermon on the Mount?** (They were frustrated; they were confused.)

● **How did you feel when I explained the clue?** (I finally understood; I should've figured it out.)

● **How might that be like the way the disciples felt when they understood something Jesus was teaching?** (They felt relieved; they probably felt like they should've known that all along.)

● **What's the most difficult thing about this activity?** (The clue was too hard; I didn't know where to begin.)

Say: **This activity was perfectly clear to me because I**

ACTION AND REFLECTION
(15 to 20 minutes)

understood the meaning of the clue. When Jesus taught his disciples and the multitudes about the Beatitudes, people may've felt like they missed some important clue. Discovering that the "poor in spirit" (those who are willing to be without worldly riches) are blessed and that "theirs is the kingdom of heaven" was probably quite a shock to these people. Jesus was teaching a new way of thinking that even today seems surprising. Let's take a closer look at the new thoughts in these passages.

BIBLE APPLICATION
(10 to 15 minutes)

WHAT'S A BEATITUDE?

Form groups of no more than three. Say: **I'm going to read aloud the section of the Sermon on the Mount we call the Beatitudes. As I read each beatitude, demonstrate the action it implies to your partners through facial expressions or pantomime.**

Kids may think this is "silly" or "dumb." Encourage them to have fun with their actions and not worry how they look to others. And, join in the fun yourself.

Read Matthew 5:1-12 aloud, pausing after each "Blessed are . . . " passage for kids to do their actions. Then have kids sit in their trios and answer the following questions:

● **Why might the people in Jesus' time have been surprised by these messages?**

● **What do the Beatitudes tell us about how we should live?**

● **What do these scriptures tell us about happiness?**

● **Does being "poor in spirit" mean we shouldn't do our best in life? Explain.**

After a few minutes, have someone from each trio tell one thing he or she learned from the discussion. Then have a volunteer read aloud 1 Samuel 16:7.

Ask:

● **How does this verse relate to the message of the Beatitudes?** (It's who you are that counts most, not what you have; God cares most about what you believe.)

Then say: **The Beatitudes tell us how to live a righteous lifestyle—a lifestyle that's pleasing to God. And immediately following this teaching, Jesus commands us to live our righteous lifestyles so others can see God's life in us.**

COMMITMENT
(5 to 10 minutes)

LIGHT OF THE WORLD

Take your kids to a room that's completely darkened (or darken the room you're meeting in). Give kids each a copy of the "Light in a Dark World" handout while they still can't see. Say: **See if you can read the message on the papers I've given you. It's an important message Jesus gave to his disciples.** After a few seconds, turn on a flashlight or light a candle to bring a small amount of light into the room. Have kids read their handouts aloud.

Then ask:

● **How easy was it to see the message when the room was completely dark?** (Impossible; I could make out some of it.)

● **How is the light I provided that helped you read the handout like the message on the handout?** (Just as the light helped us see the handout, our light can help others see God; we can be lights to help others see God's love.)

● **What can we do to be lights of the world?** (Tell others about God's love; follow the message in the Beatitudes; be good examples for others to see.)

Form a circle in the dark room. Pass the candle or flashlight around the circle as kids each say one thing they'll do to be better "lights of the world." For example, someone might say, "I will tell my friends at school about Jesus" or "I'll do my best to follow God's ways."

Say: **The Beatitudes help us see what's important in life—and how to live our lives in a way that's pleasing to God. And by sharing the message of the Beatitudes with others, we can bring light to a dark world.**

Table Talk

The Table Talk activity in this course helps junior highers and middle schoolers talk with their parents about Jesus' teachings in the Sermon on the Mount.

If you choose to use the Table Talk activity, this is a good time to show students the "Table Talk" handout (p. 21). Ask them to spend time with their parents completing it.

Before kids leave, give them each a photocopy of the "Table Talk" handout to take home, or tell them you'll be sending it to their parents.

Or use the Table Talk idea found in the Bonus Ideas (p. 47) for a meeting based on the handout.

☐ OPTION 1: PASS THE SALT

Say: **A little bit of salt goes a long way toward adding flavor to food. Jesus calls us to be the salt of the earth— that is, to season the world with his love. To close our lesson, we're going to "salt" each other with words of encouragement.**

Shake a small amount of salt into each person's hand. Then say: **Go around to at least four people and tell them each one thing you appreciate about them or their faith. As you do this, sprinkle a small amount of your salt into their hands. Relate your comments to the Beatitudes, if possible. For example, you might say, "You're a great peacemaker" or "You always show mercy to others." Be sure everyone gets at least one word of encouragement.**

When kids are done, say: **The "salt" of compliments and encouragement you shared with each other can go a long**

CLOSING
(up to 5 minutes)

way toward building up each other in faith. Let us also be Jesus' salt for the world by living out the wisdom of the Beatitudes. Amen.

☐ OPTION 2: MORE BLESSINGS

Say: **The Beatitudes tell us what's important in life. The Beatitudes describe the positive qualities we should strive for. But each of us already has qualities that make us blessed by God.**

Form a circle and have a volunteer stand in the center. Have kids in the circle tell the volunteer why he or she is "blessed" by God. Tell kids only to say positive things about his or her personality or lifestyle. For example, someone might say, "You're blessed because you're so patient" or "You're blessed because you love others." Have kids each take turns standing in the center of the circle. Then read aloud Matthew 5:13-16 as a closing prayer and challenge for kids to live out their faith.

If You Still Have Time . . .

Season of Salt—Form groups of no more than five. Have groups brainstorm ways to "salt" the world with God's love. For example, kids might think of ways to tell friends at school about God's love or ways to distribute Bibles to people who can't afford them. Then have kids choose one or two of the ideas to act on during the coming weeks.

Digging Deeper—Form study groups of no more than four to look up and discuss the following passages: Mark 9:50; Luke 6:17-38; John 13:16-17; and Philippians 4:5-9. Have kids discuss questions such as:

- ● What does this passage mean for Christians today?
- ● What's the most important lesson in this scripture?
- ● How is the message of this passage like what Jesus taught in Matthew 5:1-16?

After time for discussion, have groups report on what they discovered.

Contract
AND READING GUIDE

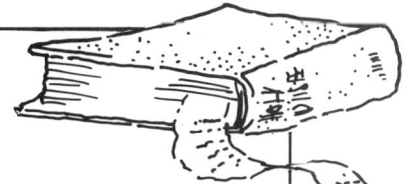

Contract

I believe that reading the Bible is an important part of my faith development. I hearby agree to read Matthew 5—7 during the next four weeks. I further agree to faithfully attend all the class sessions on *Sermon on the Mount* and, inasmuch as I am able, support and encourage others to read this book.

Signed _____   Date _____

Reading Guide

The following outline is designed to help you read Matthew 5—7 in four weeks.

Segment	Passage	Title
☐ 1	Matthew 5:1-11	The Beatitudes
☐ 2	Matthew 5:12-13	Seasoning Salt
☐ 3	Matthew 5:14-16	Light of the World
☐ 4	Matthew 5:17-20	Fulfilling the Law
☐ 5	Matthew 5:21-22	Watch Your Anger
☐ 6	Matthew 5:23-26	Reconciliation
☐ 7	Matthew 5:27-30	Lustful Hearts
☐ 8	Matthew 5:31-32	Cautions About Divorce
☐ 9	Matthew 5:33-37	Let Your No Be No
☐ 10	Matthew 5:38-42	An Eye for an Eye
☐ 11	Matthew 5:43-48	Love Your Enemies
☐ 12	Matthew 6:1-4	Secret Giving
☐ 13	Matthew 6:5-8	The Inner Room
☐ 14	Matthew 6:9-15	The Lord's Prayer
☐ 15	Matthew 6:16-18	Fasting in Secret
☐ 16	Matthew 6:19-21	Heavenly Treasures
☐ 17	Matthew 6:22-24	The Lamp of the Body
☐ 18	Matthew 6:25-32	Don't Be Anxious
☐ 19	Matthew 6:33-34	Seeking God's Kingdom First
☐ 20	Matthew 7:1-5	Taking Out the Logs
☐ 21	Matthew 7: 6	Dogs and Swine
☐ 22	Matthew 7: 7-8	Seeking and Finding
☐ 23	Matthew 7:9-11	Ask for a Fish, Get One
☐ 24	Matthew 7: 12	The Golden Rule
☐ 25	Matthew 7:13-14	The Narrow Gate
☐ 26	Matthew 7:15-20	Known by Our Fruit
☐ 27	Matthew 7:21-23	Doing God's Will
☐ 28	Matthew 7:24-29	Building on the Rock

LIGHT IN A DARK WORLD

LIGHT IN A DARK WORLD

You are the salt of the earth. But if the salt loses its saltiness, how can it be made salty again? It is no longer good for anything, except to be thrown out and trampled by men. You are the light of the world. A city set on a hill cannot be hidden. Neither do people light a lamp and put it under a bowl. Instead they put it on its stand, and it gives light to everyone in the house. In the same way, let your light shine before men, that they may see your good deeds and praise your Father in heaven." (Matthew 5:13-16).

Table Talk

To the Parent: We're involved in a junior high course at church called *Sermon on the Mount.* Students are exploring Jesus' teachings in Matthew 5—7. We'd like you and your teenager to spend some time discussing these important teachings. Use this "Table Talk" page to help you do that.

Parent and junior higher

Take turns completing the following sentences. If necessary, familiarize yourself with Matthew 5—7.
● I think the Beatitudes (in Matthew 5:1-12) are important because . . .
● What surprises me most about Jesus' preaching in the Sermon on the Mount is . . .
● One way I can put Jesus' messages into practice in my life is . . .
● If I were present when Jesus preached the Sermon on the Mount, I would've felt . . .
● The most important teaching Jesus gives in Matthew 5—7 is . . . because . . .

Talk together about the importance of prayer. Read Psalm 145:18-19; discuss the following questions:
● Why should we pray?
● What can we learn about prayer from Jesus' teachings?
● What's most difficult about praying?
● How do you feel when you see your prayers answered?

Talk about needs, concerns and joys you each have. Then spend a few moments together in prayer.

Read Matthew 5:13-16 and brainstorm three ways you can each be "salt" or "light" to the world (spread God's love to others). Then choose one of those ways to act on during the coming weeks. Hold each other accountable to your commitments.

Read together Matthew 7:24-27. Then pray aloud for each other to be like the builder who built his house upon the rock.

SERMON
on the Mount

LESSON 2

NEW LIGHT

Jesus surprised the Jews by shedding new light on the highly revered Old Testament laws. Jesus' new perspective on the old laws probably upset the Pharisees (who were the "guardians" of the Law). But Jesus' insights challenged people to look beneath the "letter of the Law" to the philosophy behind the Law. This insight can be valuable to junior highers and middle schoolers today who want to live according to God's will.

LESSON AIM

To help junior highers discover how Jesus brought a new light to God's Old Testament laws.

OBJECTIVES

Students will:
- brainstorm laws people follow or create new laws;
- follow rules for an activity and discover how it feels to break the laws;
- discover how Jesus brought new perspectives to Old Testament laws; and
- commit to follow Jesus' teachings.

BIBLE BASIS
JEREMIAH 31:31-34
MATTHEW 5:17-48

Look up the following scriptures. Then read the background paragraphs to see how the passages relate to your junior highers and middle schoolers.

In **Jeremiah 31:31-34**, the Lord describes a time when he'll make a new covenant with the house of Israel.

This passage is significant because it illustrates how God would someday put the Law in people's minds and hearts. This prophecy challenged people during Jeremiah's time to be prepared for a new way of thinking about the Law. Jesus ultimately brought that new way of thinking to the people many years later.

Junior highers and middle schoolers know a lot about rules and laws. They, like the Pharisees in Jesus' day, may be locked into trying to do just the right thing and miss the meaning behind the laws or rules. This passage can help kids see that God intends for us to write the Law in our hearts and live with a new attitude, not simply follow specific rules and regulations.

In **Matthew 5:17-48**, Jesus describes how he didn't come to abolish the Law or the Prophets, but to fulfill them.

As the disciples listened to Jesus' new perspective on the Law, they probably were astonished at his message. Jesus broadened the people's understanding of the Law. Jesus helped the people see the truths behind the laws.

It's easy to be overwhelmed by the implications of Jesus' teaching in this passage. Yet Jesus' intent was not to overwhelm people, but to help them see that the attitudes of the heart are as important as following the letter of the Law. Junior highers probably struggle with rules and laws they know how to follow, but don't fully understand. This passage can help them see that God's law is based on our desires and motivation as much as it is on our actions.

THIS LESSON AT A GLANCE

Section	Minutes	What Students Will Do	Supplies
Opener (Option 1)	5 to 10	**What's That Law?**—Play a game and try to guess various laws people follow.	Paper, pencils
(Option 2)		**The Perfect Society**—Create fictional countries and determine their countries' rules.	Newsprint, markers
Action and Reflection	15 to 20	**Follow the Rules**—Follow rules for an activity and get penalized for every incorrect action.	Paper, tape, self-stick notes
Bible Application	10 to 15	**A New Understanding**—Discover how Jesus brought new perspectives to Old Testament law.	Bibles, "Old Laws, New Perspective" handouts (p. 29), marker, newsprint, tape
Commitment	5 to 10	**New Perspectives**—Commit to follow Jesus' teachings.	"Old Laws, New Perspective" handouts (p. 29), pencils
Closing (Option 1)	up to 5	**The Law of Love**—Put one of Jesus' greatest commandments into practice.	
(Option 2)		**Thanks, Teacher**—Thank Jesus for loving us enough to teach us how to live.	

The Lesson

☐ OPTION 1: WHAT'S THAT LAW?

Form groups of no more than four. Give each group paper and pencils. Then have groups brainstorm four laws people are expected to follow. For example, someone might list "Don't speed" or "Don't steal." Then have groups each take a turn pantomiming the laws on their list for the rest of the groups to guess. After groups have guessed each law, form a circle.

Ask:

● **Was it easy to come up with four laws people are expected to follow? Explain.** (Yes, there are lots of laws in our society; no, we couldn't think of any laws.)

● **Why do we have laws such as those pantomimed?** (For safety; to keep people happy; to protect people's rights.)

● **How would you feel if someone told you that you could follow these laws exactly and still be breaking them at the same time?** (I'd wonder what the person meant by that; I'd be curious; I wouldn't care.)

Say: **Jesus brought new light to the Old Testament law people had taken at face value for many years. Jesus taught that thoughts and motives for actions are as important as following the letter of the Law. Today we'll explore what it might've been like to hear Jesus teach about the Law.**

☐ OPTION 2: THE PERFECT SOCIETY

Form groups of no more than five. Give groups each a sheet of newsprint and a marker. Say: **For the next few minutes, your groups will each be brand-new countries. You've each decided to start a new society that will not have all the problems you see in the world around you.**

In your groups, first decide on the name of your country and where it will be located. Write these on the newsprint. Then take a few minutes to decide the laws your country will have to keep it safe, happy and free from negative influences such as crime, drugs and violence.

Write each law you agree upon on your newsprint.

After a few minutes, call time and have groups each present their newsprint to the whole class. Have kids ask questions about other groups' laws if they don't agree with them or need clarification.

Then ask:

● **How easy was it to create laws for your country? Explain.** (Very easy, we didn't want many laws; very difficult, we couldn't agree on the laws.)

● **Would it be easy to enforce laws like the ones you**

OPENER
(5 to 10 minutes)

wrote? Why or why not? (Yes, our laws are easy to understand; no, we can't watch everyone all the time.)

● **Could you stop people from thinking about breaking the laws? Explain.** (No, you can't change the way people think; yes, eventually people wouldn't think about breaking the law.)

Say: **Jesus surprised many people when he taught the disciples about the well-established Old Testament law. Instead of simply restating what people already knew, Jesus taught that people's thoughts and motives for their actions are as important as their actions. In this lesson we'll explore how this new way of thinking applies to us today.**

Table Talk Follow-Up

If you sent the "Table Talk" handout (p. 21) to parents last week, discuss students' reactions to the activity. Ask volunteers to share what they learned from the discussion with their parents.

FOLLOW THE RULES

Form groups of three or four. Give groups each a supply of paper and tape. Then say: **I'm going to give you very specific rules for an activity. You must follow my rules exactly or you'll be penalized by having a self-stick note stuck to one of your group members. Each self-stick note represents one time your group broke a rule.**

Give the following instructions to the class, pausing to allow groups to complete them. If you see a group not following through exactly as you've said, penalize it by placing a self-stick note on someone in that group. Watch closely, and look for any small mistake people might make.

Instructions:

1. **Have each person in your group roll up three pieces of paper into cylinders and tape them so they won't unroll. You may not speak at all during this activity.** Penalize groups that talk or roll up the wrong number of cylinders.

2. **Stand the cylinders in a circle on the floor and tape them together to create a large circle that will serve as a base for your tower. You must all be talking during this activity until I say "stop."** Penalize groups that have quiet group members or that don't create the right kind of base as pictured in the margin. Call out "stop" before reading the next instruction.

ACTION AND REFLECTION
(15 to 20 minutes)

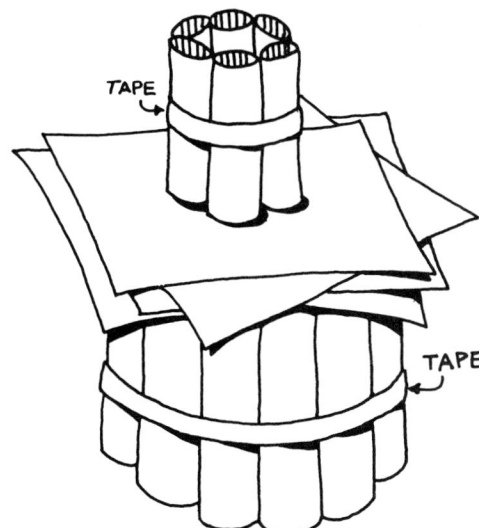

3. **Hold hands in your group and work together to lay four sheets of paper on the top of the paper base without letting go of each other's hands.** Penalize groups that don't hold hands or use the wrong number of sheets of paper.

4. **Drop hands and have each person in your group roll up and tape two more sheets of paper into cylinders, tape them together in a small circle and set them on top of the papers you just placed on the other cylinders. While you do this, you must all sing "Row, Row, Row Your Boat" until I say "stop."** Penalize groups that don't follow instructions or don't sing. Call out "stop" when kids have finished this action.

5. **Now jump up and down three times, spin in place once, do four jumping jacks, nod your head twice and shake hands with someone who isn't in a different group.** Watch closely here—you should be able to give out lots of self-stick notes.

Ask kids to look around at other groups, noting the number of self-stick notes each has. Say: **These self-stick notes each represent one time someone in your group didn't follow the rules *exactly*.**

While kids are still in their groups, ask:
● **How do you feel being penalized for making even the smallest mistake?** (It's not fair; I feel stupid; I feel angry.)
● **How did you feel as you tried to follow every rule exactly?** (I felt frustrated; I felt uncomfortable.)
● **How might this be like the way the people in Jesus' time felt trying to follow every Old Testament law?** (They probably felt frustrated; they may have felt angry.)
● **How is following these rules like following the rules we have in life?** (We have too many silly rules; some rules are hard to follow.)
● **Was it easy to follow these rules? Explain.** (No, you didn't repeat them; yes, they were self-explanatory.)
● **What was the result of following these rules?** (We built something; we created a pile of paper; we all looked silly.)

Say: **The people of Jesus' time had many rules to follow too. Some of the rules probably seemed pretty silly to the people. But when Jesus taught about the rules—the Old Testament law—he added a new dimension to the people's understanding. Let's explore that dimension by having you follow one final rule in your groups. Here's the rule: If you ever even thought once of not obeying one of these rules or that they were stupid, you must tear down your tower.**

Allow time for kids to tear down the towers. Then say: **Our thoughts and feelings are just as important as following all the rules. Jesus taught this new idea in his Sermon on the Mount—and it's still true today.**

A NEW UNDERSTANDING

Have a volunteer read aloud Jeremiah 31:31-34. Say: **Even before Jesus came on the scene, the prophet Jeremiah prophesied a time when the Law would be written upon people's hearts—when people would understand the reason for the Law and would live it in both thought and action.**

Give kids each a copy of the "Old Laws, New Perspective" handout (p. 29). Say: **A few Old Testament laws are listed down the left side of your handouts. They're important laws. But Jesus' Sermon on the Mount added a new perspective to the laws. Fold your paper in half and hold it up to a light to see the new perspective Jesus brought to the laws.** Kids should be able to read the backward writing once the handout has been folded. Allow a minute or two for kids to read the handout. See the illustration in the margin for folding instructions.

Form groups of no more than four and give each a Bible. Have volunteers in each group read aloud Matthew 5:17-48. While they're reading, list the following questions on a sheet of newsprint and tape it on the wall so kids can see it:

● How do you think the people felt when they heard Jesus' message in this passage?

● Why was Jesus' message so strong?

● What general principles can we learn from this scripture?

Have groups discuss the questions for a few minutes. Then gather together and have groups each tell one thing they learned from their discussion time.

Say: **If we took Jesus' message literally, we probably wouldn't have many eyes or hands left. But Jesus didn't intend to make more rules; instead he intended for people to live—as Jeremiah prophesied—with the Law in their hearts so it would guide not only their actions but their thoughts too.**

NEW PERSPECTIVES

Say: **Hold up your "Old Laws, New Perspective" handouts to a light again and think of ways you can follow each new perspective in your own lives. Write these next to each New Perspective. For example, you might write, "I will try not to get angry with my brother when he borrows stuff from me." Make your commitments as specific as possible. Then sign across the top of your handout as a commitment to follow Jesus' teaching.**

Form groups of no more than four and have kids each tell one thing they decided they'd do to follow Jesus' teaching.

After a couple minutes, say: **Jesus' message in Matthew 5:17-48 reminds us that we need to seek a life that's pleasing to God in both action and thought. The nice surprise is, if we commit to follow Jesus' teachings in our**

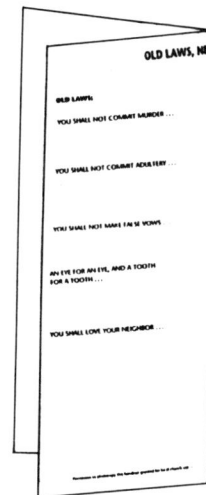

COMMITMENT
(5 to 10 minutes)

hearts, we'll naturally follow his teachings and the Old Testament commandments with our actions.

☐ OPTION 1: THE LAW OF LOVE

Form a circle. Say: **The ultimate law that Jesus teaches is the law of love. In Matthew 22:34-40, we're told to love God with all our hearts and to love our neighbors as ourselves.**

One way to show love to our neighbors is to tell them how much we appreciate their abilities and positive qualities. We're going to practice this law of love for our closing today by each saying one thing we appreciate about the person on our right.

Have kids each take turns saying aloud what they appreciate about the person on their right. Remind kids to be positive and uplifting in their comments. For example, someone might say, "I appreciate Mike's sense of humor" or "I like listening to what Sandy has to say."

☐ OPTION 2: THANKS, TEACHER

Form groups of no more than three. Say: **Jesus loved us enough to teach us how to live according to God's ways. In your group, think of a way you can express your thanks to Jesus for teaching us how to live. You might choose to create a short cheer or to form yourselves into a human sculpture representing your thankfulness.**

Allow a couple minutes for groups to choose what they'll do. Then have groups simultaneously offer their thanks to Jesus in their creative ways. Afterward, tell groups how much you enjoyed each creative action. Encourage kids to tell each other what they like most about others' thankful actions before they leave the class.

If You Still Have Time . . .

Divorce Discussion—In Matthew 5:31-32, Jesus addresses the difficult issue of divorce. Consider a discussion about this specific teaching and how it applies today. Be sensitive to junior highers who come from broken or blended families.

Gospel Parallels—Help kids dig deeper into the laws Jesus brought new perspective to by exploring Luke 6:27-39 and comparing it to Matthew 5:17-48.

Old Laws, New Perspective

OLD LAWS:

YOU SHALL NOT COMMIT MURDER ...

YOU SHALL NOT COMMIT ADULTERY ...

YOU SHALL NOT MAKE FALSE VOWS ...

AN EYE FOR AN EYE, AND A TOOTH
FOR A TOOTH ...

YOU SHALL LOVE YOUR NEIGHBOR ...

NEW PERSPECTIVES:

You've heard it said that

but I say everyone who is angry with another
shall be guilty before the court.

You've heard it said that

but I say to you, anyone who looks upon another
with lust has already committed adultery in
his or her heart.

You've heard it said that

but I say to you, make all your speech truthful.

You've heard it said

but I say, if you are slapped on the right cheek,
offer the left as well.

You've heard it said

but I say to you, love your enemies as well
and pray for those who pick on you.

LESSON 3

PRAYER

P rayer is a sensitive issue with junior highers and middle schoolers. Prayer—especially public prayer—is often uncomfortable for them. Thankfully, Jesus gave wonderful instruction on how to pray in his Sermon on the Mount. From Jesus' teaching, junior highers and middle schoolers can learn to pray confidently.

LESSON AIM

To help junior highers learn how to pray as Jesus taught his disciples to pray.

OBJECTIVES

Students will:
- discover how they feel about praying;
- explore Jesus' teaching on prayer;
- commit to improve their prayer time; and
- pray for each other.

BIBLE BASIS

PSALM 145:18-19
MATTHEW 6:5-15
MATTHEW 7:7-11

Look up the following scriptures. Then read the background paragraphs to see how the passages relate to your junior highers and middle schoolers.

In **Psalm 145:18-19**, the Psalmist reminds listeners that Jesus is always near.

This wonderful hymn of praise reminds us that God will hear our cries when we call out to him. This passage is a fitting companion to Jesus' teaching on prayer in the Sermon on the Mount as it addresses both God's nearness through prayer and God's willingness to fulfill our desires.

This passage can remind junior highers and middle schoolers that God's comfort and wisdom are only a prayer away.

In **Matthew 6:5-15**, Jesus teaches his disciples how to pray.

This familiar passage not only explains how to pray, but what we should say in our prayers as well. And while the Lord's Prayer is used in many church services, it's also intended to be used as a model for other prayers.

Your junior highers and middle schoolers may know the Lord's Prayer. But as they study the context of the prayer in this passage, they can learn how to use this as a model for their own prayers and how to approach prayer in general.

In **Matthew 7:7-11**, Jesus tells his disciples that God gives what is good to those who ask him.

This passage points out one important reason for prayer—asking God for help and guidance. It also reminds us that God wants to take care of his people by meeting their needs.

Too often, junior highers and middle schoolers are "burned" by broken promises or "help" that just doesn't come through. This passage reminds kids that God takes care of those who love him—and, while we don't always recognize it—he answers prayer.

THIS LESSON AT A GLANCE

Section	Minutes	What Students Will Do	Supplies
Opener (Option 1)	5 to 10	**How-To**—Teach each other how to do a specific thing.	Paper, pencils, cookie recipe
(Option 2)		**Reaching for God**—Discover how to reach God through prayer.	Doughnuts, tape measure
Action and Reflection	10 to 15	**Let Us Pray . . .**—Pray in a variety of ways and talk about how they feel about praying.	"How to Pray?" handouts (p. 37), Bible
Bible Application	10 to 15	**Jesus and Prayer**—Discover what Jesus taught about prayer.	Paper, pencils, Bibles
Commitment	10 to 15	**Understanding Prayer**—Discover more about prayer and commit to follow Jesus' instruction on prayer.	Bibles
Closing (Option 1)	up to 5	**Peaceful Prayer**—Pray silently while quiet music plays in the background.	Cassette player, music tape
(Option 2)		**I'll Pray for You**—Write prayers for each other.	Paper, pencils

The Lesson

☐ OPTION 1: HOW-TO

Have a volunteer come up to the front of the class. Say:
Our volunteer is going to teach us how to make cookies today. I'll give each person a sheet of paper and a pencil.

OPENER
(5 to 10 minutes)

Your job is to write down the recipe the volunteer gives you so you can make cookies sometime at home. Don't miss anything, because the cookies won't taste very good if they're missing an important ingredient. Oh, and be prepared—the steps you hear may need to be rearranged.

Take the volunteer aside for a moment and give him or her a cookie recipe. Tell the volunteer: **Read the recipe instructions out of order. Use a pencil to mark off what you've read so you don't repeat yourself. But don't read the recipe in the proper order.**

Have the volunteer read the recipe in haphazard order. Kids may get frustrated or confused by the volunteer's instructions. That's okay. Continue until the entire recipe's been read. Then have kids who think they could recite the recipe in the correct order read it and compare it to the real recipe.

After a couple minutes, ask:

● **How did you feel as you tried to follow the recipe our volunteer read?** (Frustrated; confused.)

● **How is that like the way you feel when someone gives you poor instructions or directions in real life?** (I feel frustrated; I get angry with that person.)

● **How would the disciples have felt if Jesus taught them how to pray in the same way you were taught how to make these cookies?** (They'd be confused; they wouldn't learn anything.)

Say: **Thankfully, when Jesus was teaching how to pray, his instructions were pretty clear. Today we're going to explore what Jesus taught about prayer in his Sermon on the Mount. And we'll explore how Jesus' instructions can help us learn how and why to pray.**

☐ OPTION 2: REACHING FOR GOD

This activity works best outdoors or in a room with a high ceiling. You'll need enough doughnuts for each student to have one. Form groups of no more than five. Say: **In Old Testament times, people believed they could reach God by building a tower into the sky. We're going to reach for God too, but without building a tower. The object of this game is to get as close to God as possible. You may use chairs, tables and each other to get closer to God. The team who gets closest to God will win doughnuts.**

Hold up a tape measure as if you're preparing to measure kids' human towers. Allow kids to climb on chairs and build human pyramids to "reach for God." After a few minutes, measure the height groups attained and congratulate the team that reached the highest. But don't give doughnuts to that team. If one or more teams prayed, award doughnuts to those teams. Otherwise, don't give doughnuts to anyone.

Then form a circle.

Ask:

● **What was difficult about this game?** (We didn't know exactly what to do; we couldn't reach very high.)

● **How did you feel when I didn't give doughnuts to the team who reached the highest?** (It wasn't fair; I didn't like it; I was confused.)

If one or more groups prayed, ask:

● **Why did I award doughnuts to the people who prayed?** (Because that's the way to get closest to God; because you wanted to make the other teams feel bad.)

If no teams prayed, ask:

● **Why didn't I award any doughnuts?** (Because they all reached about the same height; because you lied; because no one reached closer to God.)

Say: **I told you the object of this game was to reach the closest to God. I misdirected you by telling you how some people in the Old Testament tried to reach God. But as we all know, the way to reach God is not through building a tower or reaching into the sky, but through prayer. Not just prayer like you might have offered in this game, but an attitude of prayer you can have every day. We're going to explore Jesus' teaching on prayer and what it means for us today.**

Distribute doughnuts to people who don't have any.

LET US PRAY . . .

Say: **Since we're exploring the subject of prayer today, we'll get right into this topic by spending a few minutes in prayer. I'll give you each an instruction to follow for how to pray, then we'll get started.**

Give kids each a section of the "How to Pray?" handout (p. 37). Be sure to give the "Boastful Prayer" and "Loud Prayer" sections to kids who won't be afraid to be loud and obnoxious. If you have more than eight kids in your class, make additional copies of the handout.

After kids have read their instructions, say: **Now we'll have a three-minute prayer time. Follow your instructions and spend the next three minutes in prayer. I'll say "amen" when time is up.**

After three minutes, call time.

Form a circle and ask:

● **How did you feel when people started praying loudly or boastfully?** (I didn't like it; I was embarrassed; I thought it was funny.)

● **How did you feel about your own prayers?** (I couldn't concentrate; I felt like I was wasting my time.)

● **How is this activity like or unlike your own experiences with prayer?** (I usually don't pray this way; I don't like it when people pray aloud.)

Say: **In Jesus' time, some people were praying for all the wrong reasons. They, like our loud group members, were trying to be "holier" than the next person by**

ACTION AND REFLECTION
(10 to 15 minutes)

praying so everyone could hear them. But Jesus had different ideas on prayer, and he taught them in his Sermon on the Mount.

Have kids each tell what their handout section instructed them to do. Have someone read aloud Matthew 6:5-8. Then form pairs.

Have partners take turns completing the following sentences:
- **One way I like to pray is . . .**
- **I feel the least comfortable praying when . . .**
- **I think prayer is important because . . .**

Then have volunteers tell the whole group what they talked about with their partners.

BIBLE APPLICATION
(10 to 15 minutes)

JESUS AND PRAYER

Give kids each a sheet of paper, a pencil and a Bible. Form groups of four. Have kids in each group number off to four. Assign the following verses to the appropriate members of each group:
- The "ones" look up Matthew 6:10;
- the "twos" look up Matthew 6:11;
- the "threes" look up Matthew 6:12; and
- the "fours" look up Matthew 6:13.

Say: **As a group, first read aloud Matthew 6:9. Then take a couple minutes to read your assigned verse and rewrite it in your own words on your paper. Also write on your paper what you think the verse means for us today. You'll be sharing your ideas with your group in a couple minutes.**

Give kids two or three minutes to read and write notes about their verses. Then say: **Now you'll each have 30 seconds to tell your group members what you discovered about your verse. The Ones will be responsible for keeping track of time in each group.**

After two minutes or so, call time.

Ask volunteers to tell the whole group something they learned from other team members about their verses.

Say: **Jesus taught this now-familiar prayer as a model to use when we pray. You may have noticed certain elements in the prayer we can apply to our prayers today. Some of these elements include: praising God, asking God to do his will in our lives, asking God to meet our needs, asking for forgiveness, and asking God to help us overcome temptation. But one of the keys to understanding prayer comes in Matthew 6:6-7 which we read earlier.**

Read aloud Matthew 6:6-7 again, then ask:
- **Why does Jesus say we should pray in secret?** (Because prayer is private; so we don't sound too "holy.")
- **Do these verses tell us we shouldn't ever pray aloud? Explain.** (No, this was meant to keep people from being boastful in their prayers; no, it just reminds us that prayer is

between us and God.)

Say: **Jesus wasn't telling his disciples that public prayers were wrong. But he did make it clear that using lots of fancy words or praying so others will see how "good" you are isn't the way to pray. Instead, Jesus helps us see that prayer should be sincere communication from our hearts to God. And when we learn to pray sincerely, we will discover wonderful answers to our prayers.**

UNDERSTANDING PRAYER

Form three groups. Give two groups each a Bible. The third group won't be looking up scripture passages.

Say: **Each of our three groups will have a different assignment in this activity. The first group is to read Psalm 145:18 and come up with a short song or rap to share with the rest of the class that explains the meaning of the verse.**

The second group is to read Matthew 7:7-11 and create a short skit or pantomime that will illustrate the meaning of those verses.

The third group will spend time in prayer, asking God to help the whole class understand Jesus' teaching on prayer. This group may decide among themselves how they want to pray but must pray until time is up.

Allow about five minutes for groups one and two to work on their presentations and for group three to pray. Then call time and have groups one and two give their presentations. Allow time for questions from kids who need further clarification of the meaning of the verses.

Then say: **In this activity, as in life, we each had a different role in helping each other grow closer to God. Take a minute to go around and thank at least one person from each of the other two groups for his or her role in helping you understand more about prayer. Be specific in your comments. For example, you might say, "Thanks for doing such a good job explaining those verses to me" or "I appreciate your willingness to pray for us." Be sure each person gets at least one positive comment.**

Then ask:
● **Based on what we've learned, what can we do in our own prayer lives to follow Jesus' instruction on prayer?** (Pray often; pray in secret; pray confidently.)

Form pairs. Have kids each choose one way they'll improve their prayer time and tell their partner about their commitment.

☐ OPTION 1: PEACEFUL PRAYER

Say: **It's fitting to close our lesson on prayer with a time of prayer. I'm going to play some quiet music in the background as we each spend a few moments in silent**

COMMITMENT
(10 to 15 minutes)

CLOSING
(up to 5 minutes)

prayer. You may want to kneel or find a place in the room away from others. Remember as you pray that prayer is simply talking to God. Don't worry about saying "the right words."

In your prayer, ask God to help you follow Jesus and to better understand his teaching in the Sermon on the Mount. After a few minutes, I'll say "amen" to signal the end of class.

Play the music for about four minutes, then fade it out and say "amen." Thank kids for their willingness to participate in this class.

☐ OPTION 2: I'LL PRAY FOR YOU

Form a circle and give kids each a sheet of paper and a pencil.

Say: **To close our lesson on prayer, I'd like each person here to pray for the person on his or her right. But instead of praying aloud, we'll each write our prayer on our paper. You might want to ask God to help this person follow Jesus daily and learn more about how to pray. Don't worry about using fancy "prayer words." Just write your prayer as if you're writing a letter to God about the person on your right.**

Remind kids to be silent during this time. After a few minutes, have kids each hand their paper to the person on their right. Allow a moment for kids to read the prayers written for them. Then close by directing kids to say "amen" in unison.

If You Still Have Time . . .

Prayer Songs—Have kids look through your hymnal or songbooks for songs about prayer. Or, have kids think of popular songs about prayer.

For each song, ask:
● What's the message of this song?
● How can we apply this message to our lives?

Prayer Notebooks—Give kids each a small notebook. Have kids write their names on the notebooks and list their current prayer concerns, joys and requests on the first page of the notebook. Encourage kids to use the notebooks regularly to record their prayer concerns, joys and praises. Remind kids to follow up by noting when prayers are answered too. Consider awarding a prize to the person who has the most prayer entries by a specified date.

How To Pray

Photocopy and cut apart the following prayer instructions to give to your students.

BOASTFUL PRAYER
When you pray, pray aloud in a voice that lets others know how "holy" you are. Thank God for making you better than other people. Be boastful in your prayer as you talk about the wonderful abilities God has given you. Overdo it!

THANKFUL PRAYER
Use your prayer time to quietly thank God for all the good things in your life. Focus on recent positive events in your life.

LOUD PRAYER
Pray loudly so others can hear. Imagine you're in a big restaurant and you want to be sure everyone hears your prayer. You may want to pray about the problems in the world. Don't worry about how others feel about your loud prayers.

QUIET PRAYER
Pray silently for guidance in your life. You may sit in your chair or stand if you choose to. Concentrate on listening to God's answers to your requests.

QUIET PRAYER
Pray silently for guidance in your life. You may sit in your chair or stand if you choose to. Concentrate on listening to God's answers to your requests.

MEDITATIVE PRAYER
Spend your prayer time in silence, listening for God to speak to you. Thank God for the ability to communicate with him through prayer.

MEDITATIVE PRAYER
Spend your prayer time in silence, listening for God to speak to you. Thank God for the ability to communicate with him through prayer.

THANKFUL PRAYER
Use your prayer time to quietly thank God for all the good things in your life. Focus on recent positive events in your life.

LESSON 4

THE KINGDOM LIFE

In our judgmental society, it's all too easy for junior highers and middle schoolers to judge others. It's also easy for kids to be caught up in the pursuit of material things. Jesus' Sermon on the Mount addresses these issues in his description of what the "kingdom life"—a life pleasing to God—should be. Junior highers and middle schoolers can learn from these teachings how to better live out their Christian faith.

LESSON AIM

To help junior highers learn how to live according to God's ways.

OBJECTIVES

Students will:
● explore Jesus' teaching on material things;
● learn why it's important not to judge others;
● brainstorm applications of Jesus' teaching on living a kingdom life; and
● commit to follow Jesus' teachings.

BIBLE BASIS
MATTHEW 6:19—7:6
MATTHEW 7:13-29

Look up the following scriptures. Then read the background paragraphs to see how the passages relate to your junior highers and middle schoolers.

In **Matthew 6:19—7:6**, Jesus teaches about money, anxiety and judging others.

In these verses, Jesus describes attitudes and actions that befit people who seek the kingdom life—that is, a life pleasing to God. The disciples and the multitudes who listened to Jesus during this sermon were probably eager to hear what they must do to please God.

Junior highers and middle schoolers struggle with the issues in these verses as much as the people in Jesus' time did. They can learn from Jesus' teachings how to approach the issues of money, anxiety and judging in a Christian way.

In **Matthew 7:13-29**, Jesus describes the "narrow gate" that is at the entrance to the kingdom of God.

Jesus uses a familiar teaching style from both Judaism and Greco-Roman philosophy to compare two trees (verses 15-20), two professions of faith (verses 21-22) and two builders (verses 24-27). The essence of Jesus' message is clear: Those who truly love God will follow his ways and enter the kingdom of God.

Junior highers and middle schoolers can discover that the kingdom of God isn't something that only exists in the future (heaven). They can discover from these verses how to join the "now" of the kingdom of God. By following Jesus' teachings, kids can discover the joy and wonder of living the kingdom life.

THIS LESSON AT A GLANCE

Section	Minutes	What Students Will Do	Supplies
Opener (Option 1)	5 to 10	**Rewards**—Play a game and choose a prize of advice or doughnuts.	Wastebaskets, newspaper, markers, doughnuts, Bibles
(Option 2)		**What I Can Get**—Compete to gain the most paper clips in a specified time.	3×5 cards, paper clips, masking tape
Action and Reflection	15 to 20	**Nice Pictures**—Judge each other's artistic abilities.	Newsprint, crayons, "Art Parts" handouts (p. 45), tape
Bible Application	10 to 15	**Following God**—Discover Jesus' teachings on living the kingdom life.	Bibles, pencils, self-stick notes
Commitment	5 to 10	**Walking the Right Path**—Commit to follow Jesus' teachings.	Pencils
Closing (Option 1)	up to 5	**Treasures**—Tell each other why they're God's treasures.	
(Option 2)		**Heaven With You**—Describe what it might be like to be in heaven together.	

The Lesson

☐ OPTION 1: REWARDS

Form teams of no more than four. Set up one empty wastebasket for each team along the walls of your room. Assign teams each one wastebasket to defend. Give each team a supply of newspaper (at least 20 sheets) and a marker. Have teams each draw a symbol on their papers to identify their team. For example, one team might draw a circle on their papers; another might draw a square; still another might draw a star.

Say: **The object of this game is to score the most points. You can score points by depositing your papers into other teams' wastebaskets. You may not get closer than 3 feet to any wastebasket, whether defending your team's wastebasket or trying to score in another team's. You may not take out any papers that fall into a wastebasket. You may also throw only one crumpled-up paper at a time. You get 1 point for each crumpled paper you get into another team's basket. You get 5 points for each paper airplane you land in another team's wastebasket. But, you'll lose 1 point for every paper that ends up in your team's wastebasket, so it pays to have someone trying to block others' tosses. Once a paper misses the basket, you may pick it up and try again.**

The winner of the game will get to choose between two prizes: doughnuts or good advice. The second place team will get whichever prize is left.

Play the game for a few minutes or until all paper has been deposited into wastebaskets. Then call time. Help count the number of papers in each team's wastebasket and record this on a sheet of paper to subtract from each team's total. If kids had any of their own team's papers in their basket, discard them after subtracting 1 point for each so they won't be counted again in the final totals. Then count up the total number of each team's papers in all the wastebaskets. Award 1 point for each crumpled paper and 5 for each paper airplane. Tally the scores and determine the winning team.

Have the winning team choose the prize. It's likely they'll choose the doughnuts. If they do, reward the second-place team by reading aloud Matthew 6:19-20. If the first-place team chooses the advice, congratulate them for choosing a great prize and read the Matthew verses. Then give the doughnuts to the second-place team.

Ask:

● **How did you feel when you played this game?** (Great; happy; challenged.)

● **How is trying to win this game like trying to "win" in**

life? (The person with the most money in life wins; it's a battle to be successful in life.)

● **Which prize appealed to you most? Explain.** (The doughnuts, I'm hungry; the advice, I'm curious.)

● **How do the prizes relate to each other?** (The advice warns us not to pursue things, such as the doughnuts, that are material things.)

Say: **In this game, and in the choosing of the prizes, we've seen how we often pursue material things. Our world has taught us that the person with the most toys wins. But in Jesus' Sermon on the Mount, we discover a new perspective on treasures that can lead us to a life that's pleasing to God—the kingdom life.**

☐ OPTION 2: WHAT I CAN GET

Give kids each a 3×5 card and 10 paper clips. Have kids clip their paper clips to their 3×5 cards and use masking tape to tape their cards securely on their backs.

Say: **The object of this game is to end up with the most paper clips on your card when time is called. You can get more paper clips by stealing them off other people's 3×5 cards and reaching back to attach them to your own. You may not place your hand over your paper clips or grab more than one at a time from any one person. Keep moving to avoid losing paper clips.**

If a paper clip falls to the ground, anyone may grab it and place it on his or her own card. The person with the most paper clips when time is called will win a prize.

On "go" have kids begin the competition. After a few minutes, or when things seem to be getting out of hand, call time. Go around and count the number of paper clips on each person's card and determine the winner or winners. Give the winners each a fun prize such as a box of paper clips or a package of 3×5 cards.

Form a circle and ask:

● **How did you feel in this game as you tried to get the most paper clips? Explain.** (Frustrated, I couldn't get any paper clips; angry, people kept cheating; challenged, I wanted to win.)

● **How is that like the way people feel as they compete to make the most money or buy the best house or car?** (They feel angry because some people cheat and lie; they feel challenged to do their best.)

● **What motivated you to try to win?** (Getting the prize; I wanted to be the best.)

Say: **In our society, many people live their lives like the way you played this game—trying to get the most "things" to win. But Jesus taught a new way of thinking in his Sermon on the Mount. In this lesson we're going to explore how Jesus' teachings on money, anxiety and judging can help us belong to God's kingdom—today!**

ACTION AND REFLECTION
(15 to 20 minutes)

NICE PICTURES

Give kids each a sheet of newsprint and a few crayons.

Say: **For this next activity, we're going to exercise our artistic talents. I'll give you each a slip of paper listing something you should draw. Follow the instructions on your slips of paper carefully. You'll have five minutes to finish your drawings.**

Give kids each one section of the "Art Parts" handout (p. 45). Remind kids to work independently and not to read anyone else's slip of paper.

After five minutes, call time. Have kids each sign their artwork and tape it to a wall. Then have kids go around and judge each other's work based on how well each item is drawn. Encourage kids to be tough on each other and write comments on the drawings to indicate how they feel about how well each one is drawn. If you see kids aren't being tough enough, add your own comments such as, "Isn't realistic enough" or "Can't tell what this is." Allow a few minutes for kids to judge each other's work, then call time.

Have kids collect their own artwork and sit in a circle while they read the comments.

Then ask:

● **How did you feel as you read the comments people wrote?** (They aren't fair; angry; upset.)

● **How is that like the way you feel when people judge you?** (I don't think it's fair; it makes me angry when people judge me.)

● **Was it easy to judge each piece of art? Explain.** (Yes, I figured out each one was supposed to be bad; no, I couldn't tell what each one was.)

● **How is that like when you try to judge others based on what you see?** (It's not easy to judge others; I'm usually wrong when I judge others.)

Have kids each tell what their art instructions said.

Then ask:

● **How would your judgments have been different if you'd known what the art instructions said?** (I would've been kinder; I wouldn't have been negative in what I wrote.)

● **What does this activity tell us about judging others?** (We shouldn't judge others because we might be wrong; judging others is difficult and usually inaccurate.)

Say: **One of the key concepts in Jesus' teaching on how to live according to God's will is this concept of not judging others. This is an important teaching because it reminds us to take care of our own problems, and it helps us to be open to other people.**

Help kids tape the drawings back on the wall. Then have students go around to other kids' drawings and write new, positive comments on at least three drawings. Tell kids each drawing must receive at least one positive comment. For example, kids might write, "I like how you drew the sky" or "You did a great job of making this look bad."

FOLLOWING GOD

Say: **We've already looked at two of Jesus' teachings on how to live the kingdom life: Don't pursue material things and don't judge others. Now we'll take a closer look at these two teachings and a few more to help us know how to grow in faith.**

Form groups of no more than four. Give groups each Bibles, pencils and a supply of self-stick notes. Say: **We're going to create a "path" showing the kinds of things we can do to live the kingdom life today. Take a few minutes to read the following scripture passages in your group. Then write specific things on each of your self-stick notes that can help us do God's will. For example, we've already talked about not judging others, so you might write, "Don't judge people at school by the clothes they wear." Be as specific as possible and come up with as many practical applications of the scriptures as you can.**

Have kids list the following scripture references on one of their self-stick notes to remind them what verses they're to read: Matthew 6:19—7:6 and Matthew 7:13-29.

After a few minutes, have kids stand, facing the wall where the drawings are taped. Have kids take turns reading their self-stick notes and placing them on the wall (or drawings). The self-stick notes should be placed in a horizontal path across the wall. Tell kids it's okay if someone's already read a comment similar to theirs. Continue until all the self-stick notes are on the wall.

Ask:

● **Which scripture application do you find most challenging? Explain.** (Not judging, it's too easy to make judgments about people; not pursuing things I want, I enjoy buying and getting things.)

● **How are these applications of Jesus' teaching like a path to grow closer to God?** (If we do these things, we'll be better Christians; if we follow these ideas, we'll get to know God better.)

● **Why does Jesus describe the path to the kingdom of God as a narrow path?** (Not everyone will be in the kingdom of God; we need to watch what we're doing closely so we don't stray off the path.)

WALKING THE RIGHT PATH

Say: **Though we often think of the kingdom of God as a future event—as heaven—Jesus' teachings help us learn how we can be in God's kingdom here on earth. That doesn't mean we should separate ourselves from the rest of society though. In fact, much of Jesus' Sermon on the Mount deals with how we should relate to others. And we can help each other walk that narrow path.**

Form pairs. Have partners walk over to the wall of self-stick notes together and choose at least one of the actions

BIBLE APPLICATION
(10 to 15 minutes)

COMMITMENT
(5 to 10 minutes)

listed on the notes to follow through on in the coming week. Have students show their partners which things they'll commit to do, then initial the self-stick notes.

Say: **As we commit to do these things, we're committing to following Jesus' teachings. When you've chosen what you'll do, find a quiet place to sit with your partner and pray quietly for each other to continue to seek God's will.**

☐ OPTION 1: TREASURES

Say: **Jesus taught us that we shouldn't seek material things. But we have in this room many treasures we can enjoy—each other. As our closing today, go around to at least three people and tell them something that makes them a treasure to God. For example, you might say, "You're a treasure because you smile so much" or "You're a treasure because you're good with people." Be sure everyone gets at least one positive comment.**

When kids finish, form a circle and have kids put their arms around each other for a group hug. Thank kids for exploring Jesus' Sermon on the Mount and encourage them to study it again in the coming weeks.

☐ OPTION 2: HEAVEN WITH YOU

Form groups of no more than four. Say: **We've been talking about the kingdom life we can live today. But God has promised us a future life together too. Take a moment to brainstorm what you think heaven will be like. Then tell each person in your group why heaven will be a better place with him or her there. For example, you might say, "You'll make heaven a great place because you're always kind" or "Your humor will brighten our days in heaven."**

After a few minutes, call time and thank kids for their willingness to explore the Sermon on the Mount with you.

CLOSING
(up to 5 minutes)

If You Still Have Time . . .

Keys to the Kingdom—Have kids draw and cut out key-shaped pieces of paper. Then have kids list keys to living the kingdom life on each key. Encourage kids to keep the keys with them as reminders of Jesus' teaching in the Sermon on the Mount.

Course Reflection—Form a circle. Ask students to reflect on the past four lessons. Have them take turns completing the following sentences:
- Something I learned in this course is . . .
- If I could tell my friends about this course, I'd say . . .
- Something I'll do differently because of this course is . . .

Art Parts

Cut apart the following sections and give one to each student.

✂ --

Art Instructions:
Your job is to draw a picture of an animal—any animal. But you're to make your picture as difficult to recognize as possible. Draw poorly as if you don't know how to draw this animal. Make your drawing so bad that it will stand out when the drawings are all together.

Art Instructions:
Your job is to draw a picture of an animal—any animal. But you're to make your picture as difficult to recognize as possible. Draw poorly as if you don't know how to draw this animal. Make your drawing so bad that it will stand out when the drawings are all together.

Art Instructions:
Your job is to draw a picture of an animal—any animal. But you're to make your picture as difficult to recognize as possible. Draw poorly as if you don't know how to draw this animal. Make your drawing so bad that it will stand out when the drawings are all together.

Art Instructions:
Your job is to draw a picture of an animal—any animal. But you're to make your picture as difficult to recognize as possible. Draw poorly as if you don't know how to draw this animal. Make your drawing so bad that it will stand out when the drawings are all together.

Art Instructions:
Your job is to draw a picture of an animal—any animal. But you're to make your picture as difficult to recognize as possible. Draw poorly as if you don't know how to draw this animal. Make your drawing so bad that it will stand out when the drawings are all together.

BONUS IDEAS

My Sermon—Have kids write their own five-minute sermons based on a topic from the Sermon on the Mount. Encourage kids to be creative and meaningful in their sermons. Then have kids present their sermons to the whole class. For fun, have kids vote on the top three sermons presented and talk with your senior pastor about having these sermons presented during the regular church service.

Bonus Scriptures—The lessons focus on a select few scripture passages, but if you'd like to incorporate more Bible readings into the lessons, here are our suggestions:
- Matthew 13:44-50 (Jesus teaches about the kingdom of heaven.)
- Matthew 19:16-26 (Jesus tells a man it's easier for a camel to go through the eye of a needle than for a rich man to enter heaven.)
- Mark 1:21-28 (The people are amazed at Jesus' teaching ability.)
- John 14:1-14 (Jesus tells his disciples he will prepare a place for us in heaven.)
- Colossians 4:2-4 (Paul reminds us to devote ourselves to prayer.)
- James 5:13-18 (James encourages his readers to pray for one another.)

Heavenly Treasures—Plan a meeting based on Jesus' teaching in Matthew 6:19-24. Have kids brainstorm practical things they can do to seek heavenly treasures instead of material things. For example, kids might suggest reaching out to others, reading the Bible or helping a friend at school. Then have kids form small groups to act on some of these ideas during the rest of your meeting time.

Sermon for Today—Have kids write a skit based on some or all of Jesus' Sermon on the Mount. Then have kids perform the skit for the entire congregation during an evening program. Or, as a variation on this, have kids create a few short skits illustrating key points of the Sermon on the Mount and present them to children's Sunday school classes.

"Blessed Are" Cards—Copy and distribute the "Blessed Are" cards (p. 48). Have kids complete these cards and give them to each other as encouragement whenever they want to recognize each other's gifts and positive characteristics. Keep these cards available for kids to pick up any time. Use them yourself to affirm kids in your class.

Table Talk—Use the "Table Talk" handout (p. 21) as the basis for a meeting with parents and teenagers. During the meeting, have parents and kids complete the handout and discuss it. Plan plenty of fun activities based on the theme of the meeting. Check out *Have-a-Blast Games* (Group Books) for fun game ideas.

As much as possible, have the games and activities relate to the Sermon on the Mount. For example, kids and parents might play a game where they compete for the most pieces of candy. Then you might want to compare this to competing for the most "earthly treasures" and discuss ways we can pursue heavenly treasures.

Sermon Music Party—Plan a party based on the themes in each of the four lessons in this curriculum: the Beatitudes, Jesus' teaching on the Law, prayer and the kingdom life. Have kids help you find contemporary Christian tapes or CDs with songs relating to the topics to play during the party. Plan refreshments and give them fun names such as "Judge (K)not Pretzels," "Kingdom Pie," "Daily Bread Sticks," "Beatitude Brownies" and "Narrow Way Hot Dogs." Plan a time for kids to tell how they've applied what they've learned in the class in specific situations at school or at home.

PARTY PLEASER

Mountain Sermon Retreat—Plan a retreat near a place within walking distance of a mountain or hillside. Arrange to have all the activities and learning times done on the mountain or hill. Have kids help plan the activities and meals. Use games from *Have-a-Blast Games* (Group Books) and sing songs from *The Group Songbook* (Group Books).

For fun, have someone dress up like Jesus and sit on the hillside to read scriptures to the kids. Then have everyone discuss the scriptures and their meaning for today.

Make the retreat a fun time for kids to learn about Jesus' teachings and to enjoy the fresh air of a mountainside or hillside—as Jesus' followers probably did many years ago.

RETREAT IDEA

Blessed Are

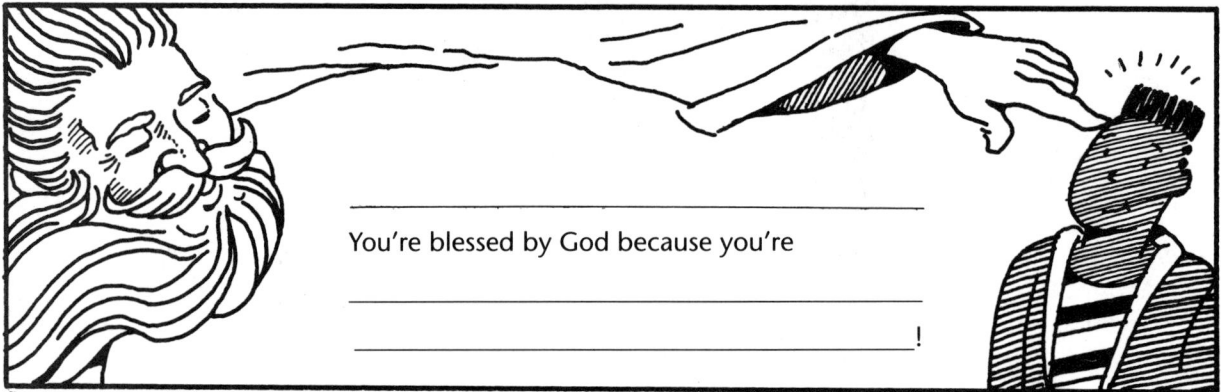

You're blessed by God because you're

_____ !

_____

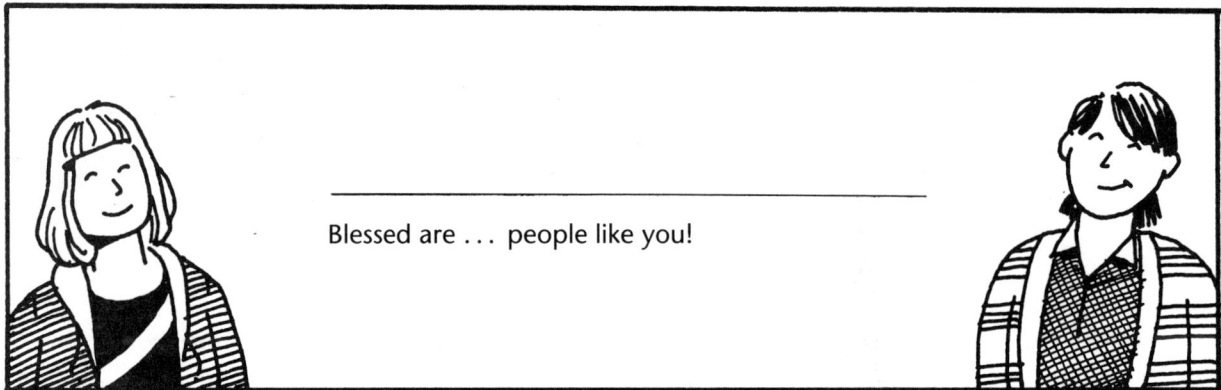

Blessed are . . . people like you!

_____

Thanks for being the salt of the earth!

Rejoice! Your reward in heaven will be great!